First Facts™

Holidays and Culture

Passover

Jewish Celebration of Freedom

by Amanda Doering

Consultant:
Dr. Kerry M. Olitzky
Executive Director
Jewish Outreach Institute

Capstone press®
Mankato, Minnesota

First Facts is published by Capstone Press,
151 Good Counsel Drive, P.O. Box 669, Mankato, Minnesota 56002.
www.capstonepress.com

Library of Congress Cataloging-in-Publication Data
Doering, Amanda.
    Passover : Jewish celebration of freedom / by Amanda Doering.
    p. cm.—(First facts. Holidays and culture)
    Summary: "Describes the history and meaning of Passover and how it is celebrated today"—
Provided by publisher.
    Includes bibliographical references and index.
    ISBN-13: 978-0-7368-6397-1 (hardcover)
    ISBN-10: 0-7368-6397-4 (hardcover)
    1. Passover—Juvenile literature. 2. Seder—Juvenile literature. I. Title. II. Series.
BM695.P3D64 2007
296.4'37—dc22   2006002949

Editorial Credits

Shari Joffe, editor; Biner Design, designer; Juliette Peters, set designer; Jo Miller, photo researcher;
    Scott Thoms, photo editor

Photo Credits

Art Directors/Helene Rogers, 12–13 (inset)
The Bridgeman Art Library, 10
Capstone Press/Karon Dubke, 21
Corbis/Richard T. Nowitz, 6–7; Roger Ressmeyer, cover, 15
Getty Images Inc./Taxi/Denis Felix, 12–13 (main)
National Council of Jewish Women of Canada, Toronto Section, 20
PhotoEdit Inc./Bill Aron, 1, 14, 16, 19
Superstock, 8, 11; age fotostock, 4–5

1 2 3 4 5 6 11 10 09 08 07 06

Table of Contents

Celebrating Passover

A **Jewish** family gathers around a beautiful table. Special foods are arranged on a plate. The family reads blessings from a prayer book. They tell the story of how Jews escaped from slavery in ancient Egypt. They are celebrating Passover.

5

What Is Passover?

Jews celebrate Passover for eight days in spring. They remember that thousands of years ago, their people were slaves in Egypt. They take pride in their Jewish **heritage**. They hope for peace and freedom for all people.

Fact!

The date of Passover changes from year to year because it is based on the Jewish calendar.

8

Living as Slaves

According to the Bible, God sent terrible **plagues** warning the Egyptians to free the Jews. But Egypt's king would not listen.

Finally, God sent an angel to kill the first-born son of every Egyptian family. God told the Jews to put lamb's blood on their doors. Then the angel would pass over their homes. This is how Passover got its name.

Fact!

The Passover story describes 10 plagues. During one plague, God turned the water into blood. God also sent swarms of flies and made Egypt dark for three days.

Freedom

After his own son was killed, Egypt's king freed the Jews. But then he changed his mind. He sent soldiers after them. The Jews came to a sea and were trapped.

God parted the sea and the Jews crossed to safety. The water then closed upon the Egyptian soldiers and they drowned. The Jews escaped to freedom.

Getting Ready

Before Passover, Jews get rid of *chametz*, bread that has been allowed to rise. Many families clean their homes until every crumb is gone.

When the Jews fled Egypt, they could not wait for bread to rise. As they traveled, they mixed flour and water and baked it in the sun. This flat **matzah** is the only bread eaten during Passover.

matzah

13

The Seder

A meal called a seder is held on the first two nights of Passover. Its steps are always done in the same order. "Seder" is the Hebrew word for "order."

A family member leads the seder. Everyone joins in. The Passover story is told. Questions are asked, songs are sung, and the meal is eaten.

An egg stands for life, hope, and new beginnings. It is also a symbol of spring, when Passover is celebrated.

Maror is a bitter herb, usually horseradish. It reminds Jews of the bitterness of slavery.

A shank bone recalls the lamb that the Jews offered every year to God to remember the night they left Egypt.

Fresh greens, usually parsley, represent spring and new life. The parsley is dipped in salt water and then eaten. The salt water stands for the tears the Jews cried as slaves.

Charoset is a mixture of apples, nuts, cinnamon, and wine. It represents mortar put between bricks. Jewish slaves used mortar while making great buildings for the Egyptians.

16

Special Foods

A special seder plate holds foods that are **symbols** of Passover. The seder leader explains the meanings of the foods. Everyone gets a taste of each food.

After the Passover story is told, a delicious meal is eaten. It may include meat, vegetables, fruit, and special dishes made with matzah flour. Many people cook **traditional** family recipes.

The Haggadah

The **Haggadah** is the book everyone reads from at the seder meal. It tells the story of how the Jews became free. It also has blessings, prayers, and traditional songs.

Fact!

Every year, the youngest child in the family reads four questions from the Haggadah about the meaning of Passover.

Amazing Holiday Story!

Every year in Toronto, Canada, the National Council of Jewish Women holds a Passover food drive. The group collects foods used during Passover. Then, food boxes are given to people who can't afford to celebrate Passover. Many homeless people, senior citizens, people with disabilities, and students are able to celebrate Passover because of this food drive.

Hands On: Afikoman Holder

The *afikoman* is a piece of matzah set aside to be the last thing eaten at the seder. At some point during the evening, the leader of the seder hides the afikoman. If the children find it, they get a reward. The afikoman is usually wrapped in a napkin or other holder before it is hidden. You can make an afikoman holder.

What You Need
8.5 x 11 inch (22 x 28 centimeter) piece of tag board
hole punch
36-inch (91-centimeter) piece of yarn
crayons or markers

What You Do
1. Fold the tag board width-wise, leaving about 2 extra inches (5 centimeters) at the top.
2. Punch holes about 1 inch (2.5 centimeters) apart around the left side, top side, and right side of the holder.
3. Decorate the holder with crayons or markers.
4. Tie a knot at the end of the yarn. Starting at the hole at the bottom left corner of the holder, lace the yarn in and out around the holder.
5. Tie a knot in the yarn after you get to the hole in the bottom right corner.

Glossary

chametz (kha-MAYTZ)—bread that has been allowed to rise

Haggadah (ha-GAHD-ah)—prayer book used during the Passover seder

heritage (HER-uh-tij)—history and traditions handed down from the past

Jewish (JOO-ish)—describing Judaism, a religion based on a belief in one God and the teachings of a holy book called the Torah

matzah (MAHT-tsa)—flat bread eaten at Passover

plague (PLAYG)—a serious disease or disaster

symbol (SIM-buhl)—a design or an object that stands for something else

traditional (truh-DISH-uhn-uhl)—passed down through time

Read More

Douglas, Lloyd G. *Let's Get Ready for Passover.* Celebrations. New York: Children's Press, 2003.

Fishman, Cathy Goldberg. *Passover.* On My Own Holidays. Minneapolis: Carolrhoda Books, 2006.

Ganeri, Anita. *The Passover Story.* Holidays. North Mankato, Minn.: Smart Apple Media, 2005.

Internet Sites

FactHound offers a safe, fun way to find Internet sites related to this book. All of the sites on FactHound have been researched by our staff.

Here's how:

1. Visit *www.facthound.com*

2. Choose your grade level.

3. Type in this book ID **0736863974** for age-appropriate sites. You may also browse subjects by clicking on letters, or by clicking on pictures and words.

4. Click on the **Fetch It** button.

FactHound will fetch the best sites for you!

Index